Finding Joy in Your Mourning
by
I.A. Young
with Shelly L. Burgess

Edited by: The PenHouse Publishing Group
Cover Design: Pearson Design

First Edition

Printed in the United States of America

Table of Contents

ACKNOWLEDGEMENTS 1

PUBLISHER REFLECTIONS 3

FOREWORD 1

FROM THE AUTHOR 1

PREFACE 1

SPRING 1

SUMMER 2

WINTER 3

WHO AM I? 5

THE DOMINO EFFECT 0

BUILDING MY SELF CONFIDENCE AND SELF ESTEEM 11

SETTING GOALS - START SMALL.... BUT START 29

TAKING ACTION 43

THE POWER OF CHOICE 50

CREATING AN IMAGE OF FAITH AND BELIEF 57

HEALING AND WHOLENESS 68

FINDING MY PLACE CALLED PURPOSE 85

DIVINE CONNECTIONS 95

EPILOGUE 103

Acknowledgements

This book is a fruitful result of love, loss, pain, and healing. It is my Heavenly Father who knows me best and found me well able to rise above whatever the world threw at me to come through every challenge victorious, empowered and healed to be a vessel that heals others.

I want to thank Reggie: This book could not have been possible without the encouragement and support you gave.

To my family: I thank you for your love and support and for never giving up on me through my journey and for allowing this book to heal.

To Shelly Burgess: Thank you for sharing your gift with me and the world. God has prepared you for greater and it's coming!!!!!!!!!

To my cover designer, Randell Pearson of Pearson's Designs: Thank you for taking my words and creating a piece that speaks on its own.

To the reader: Thank you for investing in your process and entrusting my words to promote healing, self-empowerment, and change.

Special thanks to Helen, Marlene, Tony, and Cory: This book is me finally releasing you and allowing you to rest peacefully in heaven. Each of you contributed to the person I am today, and you shared your life with me in ways that only God allowed. Thank you for it all. Until I see you again.

Publisher Reflections

At the PenHouse Group (PHG) we strive to help people tell what we call "living stories" – anecdotes that capture the essence of a human experience in a way that can help encourage, edify, and liberate others. For us, living stories never die and have the power to impact generations to come. Living stories offer insight, encouragement, hope and offer possible solutions to adverse events experienced in simply living. Every story is unique and at PHG we work closely with clients to ensure that their life story is told with integrity, relevance and meaning.

I.A. Young's story is no different. Her extraordinary life story impacted us in profound ways. The engagement and tireless hours of interviews and conversations provided us with a rare and unique peek behind the curtain of her life, thus providing inspiration, depth and understanding throughout the entire development, editing and finalization of her story. Her candid way of expressing herself provoked meaningful reflection in our own lives and impacted us profoundly in ways we will never forget. Thank you, Iris!

Finding Joy in Your Mourning is a transparent, inspiring story of resiliency, hope and promise for a fulfilling future through finding one's purpose and embracing the process to that end. It has been an auspicious honor to have worked with I.A Young. We know that all who read her story along with the companion resources, will emerge, strengthened, empowered, and fortified in the spirit, soul, and body.

Foreword
By Anisha Persaud, M.S, L.C.M.F.T

I once heard a grieving mother lament that there is no word for the loss of a child. When you lose a spouse, you are a widow or a widower. When you lose a parent, you are an orphan. But when your child dies, who are you? What do you call that? And what do you do afterwards? There is no word for the unspeakable. While death and the grief and mourning that follows is a natural part of life, we often do not associate this process with the grieving and mourning that occurs because of life adversities and other types of loss.

Believers are not promised a life free from suffering. In fact, the Bible says just the opposite, "Beloved think it not strange concerning the fiery trial which is to try you as though some strange thing happened to you: But rejoice, inasmuch as you are partakers of Christ's sufferings; that when his glory shall be revealed, you may be glad also with exceeding joy." (1 Peter 4:12-19) But how do you rejoice when your heart is so broken you must remind yourself to breathe? How do you find joy when you are too hollowed out to feel much of anything beyond the intense pain?

We intellectually accept that physical death is an inevitable and a necessary transition, but what do we do when loss of a job, a divorce or any other traumatic life event befalls us and we're the ones left picking up the pieces of what we thought our life was? As we anxiously await God's promise that "He will wipe every tear from their eyes. There will be no more death or mourning or crying or pain" (Rev 21:4), what are we to do in the meantime? How do you not simply survive tragedy, but press through to thrive?

In *Finding Joy in Your Mourning*, I. A. Young invites us to witness her journey through unimaginable loss and her life experiences that have tested the limits of her faith, patience, inner strength, and self-worth. As you read the pages of her life, she empowers us to explore our own places of suffering, disappointment, and loss to understand that at every moment in life we have a choice. We can choose to take things for granted or appreciate the good; we can choose to view failure as a catastrophe or as a learning opportunity; we can choose to succumb or make the best of what happens. When adversity hits, we can become better; we can rise above; we can even grow beyond and do things we never thought we could.

Finding Joy in Your Mourning is a real look at how joy is attainable, but that it may be found in places we never thought to look, and it may require us to do the self-work we never imagined having to do. This book lays out clear foundational principles and truths that aid the reader in rising above adversity and finding their

voice within and the strength to live life
abundantly and with purpose.

From the Author

There are many losses in life that cause us to grieve and mourn. The death of a loved one, a marriage ending in separation and divorce, being let go from a job, financial challenges, or on-going sickness. Whatever the circumstance is, we as human beings tend to live our lives by building emotional ties to people and things. When these ties are broken, lost, taken, ended, or voluntarily relinquished there is an internal struggle that occurs: a part of you tries to accept the loss, but another part of you mourns what that person or situation represented in your grand scheme of being happy and living a fulfilled life.

When we find ourselves drowning due to a profound loss, it can be difficult to escape the pain and move forward. Bernardo Stamateas, a well-known Argentine psychologist, and non-fiction Author says, *"every loss from the past that is left open becomes a burden that prevents me from taking flight and from moving forward*".

The act of mourning a loss is different for each of us. However, we must learn how to express and manage the emotions of our grief, gain insight into how it impacts our ability to learn life lessons, move forward and find our voice in the process. The important thing to remember is that your grief and mourning process and progress is necessary. Yes, mourning is painful, but it is also a process through which we overcome obstacles, grow personally and for many spiritually. Allowing yourself to go through -- the keyword here is through -- the process helps you to navigate through life with strength and with a new perspective on life.

None of us is exempt. It is something that we will all go through at some point in our lives. Anyone who has experienced a profound loss should be allowed to express his or her grief, and in some cases, this could take years to diminish because of the emotional ups and downs. Nevertheless, it is most important to underscore that the nuances and painful feelings that accompany grief are often a result of a severe, emotional injury or trauma that, like all deep wounds, will be felt, reacted to, and with work will heal in an individualistic way. However long the process, you will make it through and *"find joy in your mourning."*

Preface

For every natural experience there is a spiritual revelation but, the very first time someone told me the situation I was going through was "just a season," I had no clue what they were talking about! How could what I was feeling be a season? The more I sought God and the more I grew spiritually, I came to realize that – "a season", *had* been just that, "a season." The personal and spiritual growth we encounter moves through cycles and mirrors earthly seasons each year.

The experiences we go through in any season help develop us into better people. Like the leaves on a tree, our emotions are motivated by the "elements of life" and constantly move us up and down, in and out, to and fro sometimes leaving us challenged by our issues. Joy keeps us rooted in the knowledge of who we are, and that God is the source of strength and provision. It anchors our faith, mindset, and behavior regardless of what life brings. In joy there is a peace that surpasses all understanding during any life challenge. Each season we go through teaches valuable wisdom that ultimately prepares and matures us to provide answers to someone else's problem!

Consider if you will, that the spiritual seasons of our life could teach us lessons on healing, strength, endurance, growth, faith, and trust. Would we conduct ourselves differently? Just like nature provides a great symbolism for the peaks (*highs*) and valleys (*lows*) of life - winter, spring, summer, and fall, symbolically seem to spiritually teach us, and equip us to handle whatever life throws our way.

In the end, it is the choice to stand during your storms, going through experiences which serve as a personal process to learn invaluable strategies that will change, develop, and sustain a person throughout their life journey.

"There is a time for everything, and a season for every activity under the heavens: a time to be born and a time to die, a time to plant and a time to uproot, a time to kill and a time to heal, a time to tear down and a time to build..." - Ecclesiastes 3:1-3

SPRING

<u>**Natural**</u>: Spring is the season of new beginnings. Fresh buds bloom, animals awaken, and the earth seems to come to life again. Farmers and gardeners plant their seeds and rotate the soil; refreshing rains fall and it marks a time of transition and growth.

<u>**Spirit**</u>: The spiritual season of spring represents a time of refreshing in your mind, body, and spirit. It is a time of connecting with fresh ideas and new opportunities. It is a reset from the effects of the winter season. It is an opportunity to apply the insight gained from the winter and embrace a new perspective on life and everything around you. Spring is certainly a time of beauty and new growth! However, showers still come in nature as well as life. But God uses them to help us grow in Him, and although He does not promise us a trial or rain-free life, He does promise to be with us in the storms!

SUMMER

Natural: Summer is the warmest season of the year, falling between spring and fall. Summer is marked as a time when life seems exciting. Nature in the summer is bursting at the seams with activity. Plants typically grow best in the summer months when they receive the most sunlight and most animals are active in rearing their young and storing provisions for the winter ahead.

Spirit: Spiritual summer represents a season of adventure. It is a joyous season marked by excitement to produce and explore new ideas and concepts. A spiritual summer is a time of nourishment and strong desire to live life with passion and purpose.

AUTUMN (FALL)

Natural: Autumn is the season when leaves change color, planted seeds ripen to full maturity and the fruits of labor are seen in abundance at farmer's markets. It is the moment when the entire year's labor yields its reward. Autumn is a time of leaves falling from trees and it represents the preservation of life.

Spirit: Spiritual Autumn represents a time of harvest as well. It is a time of receiving a return on all you have worked hard to produce. This is a time of refining. It is a season of revealing growth and maturity in life. Autumn reminds us that our minds, bodies, and spirit are always developing. It emphasizes how vital it is to embrace life fully, to change, to grow and to pursue purpose.

WINTER

Natural: Nature in the winter season is marked as a long and dreary time of year. It is a time of inner growth in trees and plants and hibernation for some animals. Winter is a time of rest in preparation for the next season. One of the things I learned when researching my book and seeking to understand the seasons was that frost applies pressure to plant life to accumulate how much force will be needed for them to grow in the spring.

<u>Spirit</u>: The spiritual season of winter represents a time of reflection and introspection. it is also a time to examine your life. It is becoming self-aware of your current heart condition and motives towards others. The spiritual winter season can be hard and at times may feel isolating. But it prunes us in our attitudes, thoughts, and judgements we may make about others. It is our opportunity to cut away any unforgiveness and unhealthy relationships. Sometimes in this season, people will come into our lives to refine us and then as quickly as they come, they can go. The spiritual winter challenges our total being, forcing us to assess the pressures in our life and to take better care of ourselves. This season is a time of being still and allowing God to make changes in us. A time for strengthening up and maturing.

Chapter 1

Who am I?

Adopted. I was the youngest of six children, my father's only child and the only one given up for adoption when I was two years old. I was born in February of 1966 in the city of brotherly love, Philadelphia, Pennsylvania to an alcoholic mother and abusive, alcoholic father. One of my sister's would later recall that there were times when things seemed peaceful at home, but as soon as my parents started drinking, the fighting and arguing turned our home from a calm oasis to a chaotic warzone. My biological mother Helen had her first drink at the age of 10 and her last at the age of 60. The only memory I have of my biological father John was him drinking. The few times I did see him he was drunk. As I think about it, I never saw him sober.

My mother, Helen and the woman who would later adopt me were childhood friends. My father, John was approximately 12 years older than my mother Helen, when they married. He was also the blood relative – an uncle to be exact of my adoptive mother, Marlene. You see, Marlene's mother Elaine and my father John were brother and sister, biologically making Marlene my first cousin. As if this couldn't get any more confusing, my father John's mother would later take in and raise Marlene, at the age of seven years old after her mother died. This complex evolution of loss, relationship and divinely inspired connections would later work together very intricately unveiling a plan that would ultimately lead me to finding my peace, my joy, and my purpose during my mourning.

As with most friends, time went by, and my mother Helen and Marlene's lives took very different paths. They didn't see each other often but it would be the trust that bonded their friendship that would lead Helen to later seek out her childhood friend to make one of the most difficult decisions she would have to make in her life. She was desperate and sought the compassion of her childhood friend to make a life-changing and, possibly, life-saving decision. This would be my mother Helen's last shot at doing something right as a mother, when the decisions she had made for her other children weren't her best. She was faced with a dilemma that required an immediate solution.

Her answer would arrive one day in 1968 when her childhood friend came to Chester, Pennsylvania for a visit. The visit began with two childhood playmates getting caught up on life and good times past. But the focus of their conversation quickly changed. After what seems like hours reminiscing about the past, Marlene observed her friend's daughter playing with her sister.

"What a cute little girl," Marlene noted remembering the personal history of my life.

Helen responded bluntly, "Do you want her?"

It was this visit and conversation that would orchestrate a chain of events that would later make my cousin my mom. Due to her own loss, addiction and life traumas, my mom was at a place in her life where she simply could not take care of herself let alone manage the responsibility of caring for six children. Caught off guard by the question, and thinking her friend was joking; Marlene would soon find out how very serious my mother was. Married with no children of her own at that time, Marlene didn't give an immediate answer. What she did say with a puzzled expression was "let me talk to Skip about it." Marlene knew this was not a decision to be taken lightly, and to agree to take on the responsibility of raising her uncle's child would not only change my life but she and her husband Skip's life as well. It was a simple, but complicated decision for them with serious consequences.

By this time my older siblings, Emmanuel, Maria, and Teresa had been removed from our home by Child Services and were living with our maternal grandparents. My brother Christopher was the 4th child born to my mother and by the time he was two years' old he had been left on the doorstep of his father's home by our mother. My brother Chris and I were seven years apart and we would not find out that each other existed until I was well into my 40's. This left my sister Rosalee (Rosie) who was a year older than me and myself as the only children still at home with our mother and my father John, leaving our fate in the hands of the Philadelphia foster care system if no one from the family quickly stepped in.

I can only imagine what Marlene's ride home from Chester was like -- swirling thoughts, feelings, and concern for the little girl she had just encountered. But in the end, Marlene handled Helen's unexpected question much like she did most things in her life – with focused determination to do what she felt was right.

Upon arriving home, the discussion began but in Marlene's mind the decision was already made.

"Skip, we have an opportunity," she declared.

And without hesitation he responded that "if raising your uncle's daughter is what you think is best then that is what we will do." The decision was made. Cousin Marlene and Skip would soon become my mom and dad.

It is unclear how my siblings initially found out that I was going to be adopted. But my sister Rosie remembers she and I playing as little girls and then sometime later me being gone. Shortly after Marlene and Skip brought me to

Washington, D.C., Rosie was taken from our mother and raised by an older cousin. I can only imagine what sadness she must have felt being a young child herself. As I grew older my longing for my family caused a form of grief; leaving me to wonder…. I had questions. Many questions. Why was I given up for adoption and my other siblings were not? What did I do wrong to cause them not to want me anymore? Why didn't my parent's love me? After the adoption was finalized, I would experience mental, emotional, and physical challenges that would follow me well into adulthood.

For as long as I can remember I always knew I was adopted. I knew that I had a whole other life and family which included brothers and sisters. This transition was difficult for me being the youngest of 6 to now being a child of one alone with strangers. This made me sad and at times very angry. Family members on my father John's side felt that it was important for him to be able to see his only child even though he was in no position to father me. I remember I would occasionally get to see my biological parents during annual holiday visits at my aunt's house in Camden, New Jersey. But I was never allowed any communication with my mother's side of the family until later in life. The family dynamics of alcoholism were prominent on both sides of my family. My most vivid memory of those visits were my mother and my father drinking and arguing with one another. Even now talking about it triggers in me the distinct smell of sweat, alcohol and cigarettes coming from their pores when they hugged me. Marlene would later say that these visits were too much for me emotionally because it would take days to get me back to what they saw as my normal self. For that reason, Marlene and Skip got to a point where they felt it was in my best emotional interest to cut-off access and communication with my biological parents, altogether. I would not see my birth parent's again until my father John's funeral. I was nine years old and during the repass following his funeral it would be my first time seeing my siblings since I had been adopted. I would be almost 20 years old before I would see them again and as for my mother, Helen, I would not see her again until I was 24.

Over the years my sister Rosie tried to keep in touch and would write to me from time to time. On one occasion, she put her phone number in a letter, and every now and then I would sneak to call her. But as soon as Marlene found out, even that brief attempt to connect with my family was cut off. I believe it was Marlene's attempt to preserve a sense of normalcy and stability in my life, but I also believe it was her way of keeping control. There were several times growing up that Marlene would say "if you don't do what your told you will wind up just like Helen." Not fully understanding what that meant It scared me enough to obey whatever she was admonishing me about at the time. I felt like I was supposed to act as if my birth family didn't exist -- which in my mind made me feel as though I didn't exist either.

It wasn't until my late teens, early twenties, that under a cloak of secrecy was I able to meet and spend time with my maternal grandparents as well as my brothers and sisters. I was grateful for those stolen moments because my siblings share childhood memories with me. At one such visit; my sister Rosie would later recall how she use to get on the MARC train to visit family members on the Eastern Shore during the summers. While on these trips she would look out her window and see cargo trains going by and asking if I was on them. She believed that if she could get off her train and get on the train passing by in the other direction, she could see me. Hearing her share that memory takes me back to the look she had on her face when she shared it with me. What a sense of sadness she must have felt knowing I was never coming home.

Growing up I did all the things little girls typically do. I took dance classes, played with baby dolls, and the toys were plentiful at Christmas. We weren't rich but I didn't want for anything materialistically. I would grow to understand that what I needed most as an adopted child was to feel and be told that my adoption was not out of pity but rather it was a true act of love. I needed re-assurance that there was nothing I did wrong to bring about my fate. And that everything was going to be alright despite what happened. There were periods of happiness in my childhood, but I also remember being sad, at times angry and crying myself to sleep a lot. I didn't feel like I fit in anywhere. I often wondered "who am I really?" As a child I felt like a throwaway. I missed my siblings and wanted to be with them. I had a gaping hole within me, and I didn't know how to close it. A part of me was missing and I could do nothing about it, or so I thought. My questions never seemed to end in my mind. Why was I born if I was going to be given away? Where did I get my peculiarities from? Where did my creative desire and abilities come from? I've always loved writing poetry. Why did I love it so much? I wondered. I also knew nothing about my family's medical history which would later prove to be critical information because of the health challenges I would experience later in life.

Marlene and Skip eventually had a child of their own and I was excited about becoming a big sister. Finally, someone I could bond and play with? No. When we were younger, my little sister and I didn't get along at all. I felt as though I was constantly being measured by who she was and what she was doing. She was an honor roll student, a star athlete; the golden child in my mind; which reinforced my internal insecurities and questions of, "who am I?" Even though I was the oldest, I always felt like I was walking and existing in her shadow. The sibling I was excited to have and wanted to connect with became the proverbial thorn in my side and in my mind another source of loss, rejection, and abandonment. Yet, the feelings we had about each other were by no means by our own design. We were innocent and entrenched in a controlling environment where individuals didn't know how to heal from the emotions of their own past traumas and feelings of loss.

As an adolescent I didn't have a lot of friends – I was teased and bullied a lot and the people I considered friends, I held onto tightly. I was awkwardly introverted and fearfully shy. I didn't challenge myself to do much of anything because I didn't think I could succeed. I felt as though there was nothing about me of value to offer the world. I constantly struggled with negative thoughts and believed I was ugly and dumb. I didn't think I had anything to say that would be of any interest to anyone. These feelings of low self-esteem and inadequacy made me a chameleon and a follower to mask my pain. My need to belong caused me to be easily influenced and taken advantage of.

I grew up fearing my mother and often gave in to her telling me how incapable I was. I heard it so often that it became easier to "comply rather than try." I remember her saying to me "you don't have an original thought unless I give it to you." These words were like daggers to my soul and crippled any attempts on my part to think for myself or believe in my own self-worth.

Now my dad Skip was my shield and my greatest supporter. He was the one who gave hugs and told me he loved me. My dad spoke with me, not at me and he always spoke in a calm, soothing and reassuring voice. But everyone in the household was trying to be heard and struggling to find their own sense of freedom from Marlene's demands and expectations. This sometimes left me fighting alone against my mom's stern ways. I realize now that my mom Marlene loved me the best way she knew how, but − it was her way or no way. She administered tough love. It was black or white but never grey. This was a challenge for me because I needed her to hear me and show me love. I needed my mom to teach me how to not be afraid of everything. I needed to know that I had a choice to decide whether my sadness and anger would control and define my life moving forward. It was a constant fight. But more than that, I was struggling internally from being forced to conform into someone I knew within my heart I was not. Years later, everything Marlene said I was incapable of doing; I set out on a mission to do and be. It didn't just happen overnight. It was a constant struggle with self-destructive and self-defeating behaviors, but I made up my mind to push through.

The environment we grow up in lays the foundation we build our core values upon. It teaches us how to be resilient or how to struggle emotionally in tough times. I was trying to grow and develop in an environment that would not allow or sustain who I was and needed to be. Everyone was living on autopilot.

As I continued to evolve during my teenage years, most decisions were made for me not by me. For that reason, I didn't challenge myself to freely think for myself. I relied more on what Marlene would think or say for most of my life.

In 1983, I graduated from Frederick Douglass Senior High School in Upper Marlboro, Maryland and immediately was enrolled in

community college and began taking courses —
courses my parents picked for me. I had yet to
learn any skills that would teach me how to trust
my own judgment or make effective decisions on
my own. I was walking through my life just
"doing" and not questioning how or why -- trying
to make it from day to day existing and getting
through each day unscathed.

Now, I did enjoy behavioral sciences,
psychology, and sociology because it helped me
gain insight into the why and how of a person's
thought processes and behaviors. Math and
science however were a struggle for me. Being told
how to think and what to do never taught me how
to use critical thinking and basic problem-solving
skills once I became older. All I was required to do
was not ask questions and comply with all parental
directives. This way of thinking reinforced my
own painful belief that I was not smart, a

disappointment and incapable of measuring up to anyone's expectations or standards.

By my 20's I was still living at home and had reached my breaking point. I was tired of being controlled by my emotions and the opinions of others -- especially my mom. I started denying the narrative created for me. I started rebelling and fighting for my independence, my freedom and acceptance of my own voice. If I was going to find out who I was then I was going to have to raise up from my depression, my guilt, and my pain to take a leap of faith and start the process of empowerment, healing, and growth.

I was reunited again with my biological mother Helen in my late 30's. She became ill and was diagnosed with stage 4 cancer. She used the last 2 years of her life to live in the present. She chose to forgive herself and no longer mourn her past. In doing so, she found peace and a joy that allowed her to be reconciled with all six of her children. As a family we were able to heal and find forgiveness with our mother in the middle of mourning her death.

From adoption to adulthood, my life journey of grief and loss began at an early age and has remained present for a significant part of my life. From that casual meeting of a stranger as a little girl to the woman I am today writing this manuscript, I have overcome many different forms of grief and loss. But through all of it I have gained an awareness, a joy, and a peace in knowing that there were benefits in going through my process. I lost a lot, but what I found was me. I believe it was God using my life experiences to strengthen and build me into a masterful creation setting me on a path that helped me find my place called purpose. Who am I? I was Iris Naomi Jackson. I was Iris Annice Abbitt. I was a widow, and a mother. Today, I am Iris Annice Young.

Chapter 2
The Domino Effect

Tony and I went to the same high school. He and his sister Cheryl were good friends of mine. I would hang out at their house sometimes and it was there Tony, and I would talk and joke around only to find out that we had similar experiences growing up. There were many times when we would talk about things we were going through in life and relationships. Tony lost his mother and grandmother to cancer within a year of each other and he was doing his best to help provide for and spend time with his son from a previous relationship. The running joke between us became, "nobody understands us but us, so we need to just be with each other."

But somehow, somewhere along the way it stopped being a joke between us and we began dating. We had a lot of things in common and we were both living with disappointment. We talked a lot about how we felt like we weren't measuring up to our parent's expectations and not living the life we wanted for ourselves.

Tony and I had been dating for a short while when I soon found out I was pregnant. Both of us were living at home with our parent's and neither of us had jobs that could financially support us living on our own. Unfortunately, I would not be able to carry our baby to full-term. I miscarried in my fifth month. That loss was a devastating time for me and once again there was something I wanted so badly being taken from me. But this would not be the last time I found myself going down that road. The silver lining for me was that I had Tony and he had me. I think back on it now and realize that in some ways Tony was rescuing me just as much as I was rescuing him, and we loved each other for it.

Shortly after losing our baby, Tony had been accepted into the United States Coast Guard and in August of 1991 we were married. I was 27 years old. By November of 1992, I gave birth to our son Cory. I was finally happy. All I ever wanted at that time in my life was to be a wife and a mother and I felt like God had answered my prayers.

Tony was temporarily stationed out of state and was able to come home every other weekend when he wasn't at sea - this lifestyle forced me to step up. The things I was told and believed I was incapable of were now the things I had to figure out on my own. By marrying Tony, it positioned me to find some value in myself as well as a sense of independence. He saw in me that which I didn't see in myself. But our happily ever after would not last. Once again heartbreak and grief would cross my doorstep. All that I thought I was and all that I thought I would be was about to change forever.

Trauma and loss are the matches that ignite the grief and mourning process. It's difficult enough dealing with one such event. But what about experiencing one hit after another creating a domino effect? Not just someone dying but the loss of anything we find ourselves emotionally and mentally tied to. The accumulation of loss and unprocessed emotion in succession is called *"cumulative grief."* This compounding of events can cause you to react in unhealthy ways and make you feel as though the pain of it all is too difficult to get through or move forward. Suffering multiple losses in this manner can cause grief overload, emotional numbness, and give you a sense of not knowing where or how to begin to cope, grieve and heal.

When my husband Tony died, I was traumatized, and cumulative grief would become a very real part of my life journey. Tony had come home for the weekend from his Coast Guard post on Governor's Island in New York City to celebrate Mother's Day with our son Cory and me. That Sunday after visiting with family I took him to the train station so he could head back to the Island for the work week ahead. He called me later that evening to let me know he had returned safely. We exchanged our "I love yous," and hung up. Knowing he was ok, Cory and I settled in for the night. Monday began like any other. I had settled into my routine of picking up and dropping off the baby at daycare, going to work and coming home to fix dinner, settling Cory in bed, and preparing for the next workday. By Tuesday evening, my routine life was about to be turned upside down.

As I was preparing dinner, the phone rang. The voice on the other end introduced himself as a Coast Guard commanding officer. With a short quick breath, he told me that Tony had a medical incident, he was unresponsive and that he had been rushed to St. Vincent's Hospital in Manhattan. Not sure if I had heard him correctly,

I asked him to repeat what he had said. He told me again and said that he had no other information and asked me to hold off making any travel plans until he could get more details regarding Tony's condition. Immediately I called my best friend Patty and her husband who lived next door. I was in a state of fear and confusion. Of course, I was not waiting for any call back before deciding to rush to Tony's side. As family members quickly arrived, my parents took Cory home with them. and my father-in-law and I decided to catch the red eye to New York not knowing what awaited us. I don't remember the ride to the airport or the flight for that matter. What I do remember was the moment the pilot announced we were in New York airspace; at that very moment I felt a cold breeze go straight through my heart. It was then I knew that my husband was never coming home.

By the time we landed, my father-in-law and I were greeted by two men in uniform. One of which I would soon find out was a Chaplin. As we arrived at the hospital, we were quickly taken to a private room where we were met by a team of emergency room doctors. They tried their best to prepare me for what I was about to see. No one can prepare you for that. As we approached the bed, my heart felt like it was beating right out of my chest. Then suddenly the curtain was pulled back, and I hit the floor screaming, crying, and bargaining with God that if he would let Tony be alright I would do just about anything. He had suffered a severe brain aneurysm and he was in a coma. Tony was admitted to a private room, and I sat with him around the clock telling him he was a fighter and how much I loved and needed him. I prayed and read Psalms 23 repeatedly, only leaving his side to go to the restroom. But, two days later my worst fears would be confirmed.

Tony had no brain activity. A once strong, healthy, active young man would forever remain in a vegetative state with the use of a machine to make every breath and it was now up to me to make the decision whether to take him off life support. I was 27 years old. We had been married for 1 ½ years and our son was almost 18 months old. At the age of 30 Tony Young was gone.

I consciously grieved Tony's death for eight long years. It was so bad that my parents had to take Cory for a while because of my depression and drinking. I would later discover that the only thing that would lift from me the grip of my grief was tapping into a spiritual place. So, I stopped drinking, started going to therapy and re-dedicated my life to Christ. My healing process was about to begin.

As the years went by Cory grew up and we settled into our new normal. I was changing, I was growing, I was healing. Even though I continued to make mistakes and learn from them, I stumbled and sometimes fell but I always got back up! I had to keep it moving because Cory needed me. Yet again, years later my life would take another hit and send me down a familiar road.

The year was 2016. Cory was working and living at home. This next storm would begin with me taking a trip to the emergency room followed by the next 10 months marked by 5 specialists, weekly doctor's appointments, multiple diagnoses, countless medication -- fifteen at one-time to be exact – every possible diagnostic scan you can think of endless blood tests and treatments. Two surgeries. The first one removed a piece of my right lung and the other left one side of my vocal cord permanently paralyzed. I would have to learn how to talk and swallow again.

By August of that same year, Cory died at home from a heart arrhythmia. He was 23 years old. I was sick, alone and had to bury my only child. By October I was severely depressed, unable to work and out of medical leave. I would not be able to go back to work anytime soon in the foreseeable future. My car and rent were months behind, and my other bills were stacking up. I was in serious financial trouble and my widow's pension was the only money I had coming in and that alone was not going to be enough to live on. As if that wasn't enough, by January of 2017 my condo building caught on fire leaving me sick, unemployed, homeless, grieving and living on my sister's couch for the next 1 ½ years fighting for disability. Ten-months, all that non-stop, back-to-back for ten-months! My journey of grief, mourning and loss was a long one, but the pain of grief did eventually go away. My mourning process was longer and took me on a journey of self-discovery, healing, wholeness, and change. Everything I've been through taught me how to "grow" forward – the active process of change. I did my self-work. It was hard but it taught me that all this time I'd been existing not living because I had always been in survival mode. Waiting for one trauma after another to hit my life. I was determined to get healthy and whole in every area of my life and it would be done from the inside out. I wasn't just grieving things outside of me what I found was I was grieving me from who I thought I was to the person I know I am today.

Chapter 3
Building My Self Confidence and Self Esteem

It's one thing to think you know who you are by the role you fulfill, but your life role doesn't capture the true essence of who you are as a woman, a sister, a daughter, a friend, a spouse, a mother, or colleague. It doesn't define who we are as human beings. Our life roles simply identify a piece of us. Deep down within my soul I knew there was more to who I was going to be outside of being a mother and a wife. When someone is grieving a loss, any loss, it causes a few things to happen. First it causes you to question your life purpose. Then, it causes you to reflect on who you are and lastly, it causes you to re-evaluate what's truly important in life. Over time I would realize that my grieving process was going to help me figure out who I was created and purposed to be in the earth -- if I was willing to go through the process.

Process of Change

My process of change started with a choice that eventually got me to a place in my life where my wondering became a mission of self-discovery. If I wanted to think different, live different and be different, I was going to have to do something different. I realized I could no longer rest in my self-defeating comfort; nor could I allow my fear to overrule truth and destiny. I had to turn off my automatic pilot and get back in the driver's seat and drive! Destination unknown.

Our self-esteem and self-image are rooted in how we feel and see ourselves. I knew my change would have to begin by seeing myself in a more positive light and this required me to have to change my way of thinking. For me this began when I turned off my autopilot. I stopped doing what I always did without thought or questioning why. I became self-aware of what I was speaking, thinking, and doing. Each day I would identify one thing that made me feel good about myself. I did this day after day until my thoughts began to change, and I began to see myself differently and feel hopeful. I had to believe what I was saying until I could see it. Affirmations were also helpful to get me to replace reactive negative thoughts with positive and proactive new ones.

Some days were easier than others, but it is something I still practice today to maintain my resilience when life challenges come. Every evening before I went to bed, I would reflect over my day and find the one thing that brought me joy. Then I thought about one thing I could look forward to doing the next day. Big or small it didn't matter. The goal was to be mindful. I had to show up every-day and exercise gratitude. By changing my focus from what I didn't have to what I had and from what wasn't to what was.

This was the way I began to build and improve my self-esteem. My nightly mental activity of identifying "the one thing I liked" was an important first step in becoming confident in who I was. I committed to that first step as I knew I wouldn't become super woman in mind and action overnight. This was a baby step of many steps to come.

The process of change is like an onion. It can produce or evoke many tears. Let's dig a little deeper. When you begin to cut an onion, you peel it layer by layer. In between those layers is a very thin film that you may not see unless you pick at the layer you cut. Our self-awareness is a lot like those layers within the onion. Our change process happens layer by layer. First, you can see the obvious things about yourself, but it is when you cut deeper into the onion picking away the layers that the hidden stuff (thin film) gets exposed. On an onion the film is called "scales". Your scales reveal those things within you that aren't as obvious, and it is in this revelation the hard work begins. Hidden layers of your true self get exposed for you to cut away the bruised parts of your life journey that cause you to produce bad fruit or no fruit at all. Exposure of hidden layers within you enables you to face your challenges and deal with them to heal, to forgive and to grow to a place you never imagined you were able to see. It was during a conversation with a friend recently that I realized that most of my adult life I have been in survival mode, living one day to the next, not really understanding or processing the "whys" of how I do it, but just trying to make it through each day. This is the autopilot I was speaking of earlier. I'm thankful to be at a place now where I am mindful enough to appreciate the little things in life and that I'm living in a way that allows me to experience joy while I'm living it. I was existing before. But now I live and I'm present.

The fact is, when we experience loss - it can seem as though we are just trying to "make it through" in life. We experience pockets and moments of happiness but no real joy. Now, for me, true joy is present and alive regardless of what is going on in my life. I now know that I can get up, press forward, and move on regardless of what happens in my life because I'm rooted in truth of who I am. I am not defined by my experiences. Though they may impact me, they do not dictate who I am to be, how I show up and how I interact with others. I am no longer ruled by emotions that leave me side-tracked, derailed, or even stuck.

I can tell you that my own self-discovery is ever evolving but my self-esteem has improved. From looking for something every day to feel good about myself to truly building up my own self-worth and value, I focus on accepting small victories that lead up to big ones. Instead of the things I might not have gotten right or could have done better. I celebrate showing up daily and trying. It all boils down that on those days when showing up might be a challenge, I choose to do something despite how I feel. This is about self-care; making sure that I'm doing whatever I can do to take care of myself mentally, physically, spiritually, and emotionally. And sometimes, that requires rest. But we can't get stuck in rest, we must get up and keep moving forward.

Managing my Comfort Zone

It goes back to the onion. It is another layer of self-discovery. When you are uncertain or not comfortable in your own skin or self, you talk yourself out of exploring those things outside of your comfort zone. Within your comfort zone you can determine the level of pleasure or pain that comfort produces, and you teach yourself how to navigate through it with acceptable consequences. It's familiar. But when you are out of your comfort zone, you must learn to go through the flow of it. You must be willing to experience some temporary discomfort to learn new things and gain wisdom for life-long gain.

So how do I maintain and continue to build my self-esteem and self-confidence? First, I had to stop surrounding myself with people who shared my problem and started surrounding myself with people who had my answer. Everyone remembers the adage, "misery loves company." I had to stop allowing people to embrace my "woe is me." I needed people to challenge my negative thinking and to challenge me to get up. When you are in an emotionally charged place, you really don't want to hear people come with the silver lining. I had to get to a place where I realized that everyone, I was trying to hold onto wasn't willing or supposed to come along. Not only was I hurting myself dragging people into my growth process, but I was potentially putting them in a position to shipwreck their own self-discovery journey.

When we step outside of our comfort zone, it affords us the opportunity to connect and develop new relationships and have new experiences that uniquely add and further our lives.

Working My Wall

I had to get to the place where it didn't matter what people thought or said because their opinion didn't mean it was necessarily true. Problems can seem overwhelming and endless in life because of the lens we use to see our situations. Just because someone has an opinion doesn't mean I have to embrace it as truth for my own life. It's just that, an opinion.

Consider this, what if I told you that your problem was in fact not a problem but a process? And what if your difficulties or weaknesses were actually opportunities? Would it change the way you see your situation? Would you approach it with a different mindset and attitude? Almost all of us at some point in our lives have been imprisoned behind a proverbial wall of our false beliefs and bad experiences. They have framed our views, justified our behavior, and skewed our core values to keep us from having to feel and re-live the painful experiences from our past. These walls we create are often regarded by us as protection but the purpose they serve is a limiting survival mechanism.

When I was a treatment coordinator at the Prince George's County Department of Corrections, I facilitated a women's empowerment group. In this group, participants were given an exercise entitled "Working My Wall." In the exercise, participants were asked to think about their proverbial wall (s). The ones that we all sometimes hide behind to ensure our emotional protection from past hurts or trauma. First, I asked them to visualize how high their wall was. Next, I asked them to visualize how wide their wall was. Then I asked them to visualize all the personal vows and situations they were protecting themselves from behind their wall. Finally, I asked them to visualize themselves behind their wall with all that stuff. Boom! We believe that by creating our walls we are protecting ourselves, but the reality is that we are creating a barrier to our change and growth process. I had the women in the group think about each brick on their wall which represented a statement or vow such as "I'm not going to be hurt like that again" or the example of a woman who says, "all men are dogs." The reality is your wall does not really protect you because you are behind it with all that stuff. So, nothing good can come in and nothing bad can go out. But there is a way to knock your wall down and you start one brick at a time. As you become more self-aware, you may be able to knock down multiple bricks.

How?   By acceptance, forgiveness, understanding, and greater self-love.   For example, I always believed until I was told differently, that my biological mother didn't want me, which made me feel like I was worthless and unlovable. I was able to knock that brick down, when my mother came to live with me as an adult. She was able to share the reasons behind her decision to give me up for adoption and not my other siblings. I was able to understand and accept that it really had nothing to do with me being lovable or not. It was a decision she had to make for my safety and for a better life for me. So, after years of harboring unforgiveness towards my mother, I was able to let go of that false ideal and perception of my mother giving me up. "Living life" causes us to create walls, high and wide, but these walls cannot stand if we truly wish to be free and change the way we live our lives.

Growing up I didn't challenge myself because of the words my adoptive mother spoke to me. I didn't think I had anything of value and my wall was created out of my pain, denial and her sometimes speaking false truths. Our mind is a powerful thing and like a computer what we put into it is what will come out of it. What is processed into our thinking and feeling outputs how we behave. In my mind I had to overcome thinking that I wasn't smart enough. Those words and others like them would play over and over like an old record stuck in a groove and would continue to play well into my 20's and 30's. I had to take the needle off the record and change the tune.

As I shared in the previous chapter, from an early age, I was fighting for my voice and freedom. Daily arguments with my adoptive mother were the norm. I later discovered after her death there were childhood traumas that left her guarded and may have been the cause of her harsh nature. Her wall was thick, and it allowed her the comfort of not having to express much emotion. My mom's wall created the lens by which she saw the world. It was like a repellent. Knowing what I now know about her, I believe the little girl she adopted became the reflection of her childhood fears, insecurities, and sadness and rather than confront and heal her own trauma she sought to eradicate any resemblance of her younger self seen in me.

Understanding makes a difference in life. How I grew from that was difficult, but I was able to accept her because I now understood her. I had to learn that the longer I tried to focus on why Marlene was the way she was I could not become self-aware of my own growth process and the need to change self-defeating behaviors and how to change them. Your parents or whomever raised you could only do what they were taught. If fear, trauma, abandonment, neglect, or rejection was their life experience, they processed it at whatever age it happened. Without the understanding of proper coping skills, traumas like these go unaddressed and develop into dysfunctional, self-defeating behavior. A child no matter how bright, can only process information at the level of their mental capacity. You were not and are not the problem! You may have been a reflection or reminder of their own fears, insecurities, and inability to have control over that which controlled them.

Life Roles That Define Us

Role playing is something that most people have done at different times in their life, either for fun or for survival. For example, as an adult, defining myself as a wife or mother and all that those roles required; was how I defined my worth and value. But when those roles were changed or challenged due to unforeseen circumstances whether it was tragic or not, I started thinking about who I was outside of those roles.   I had to figure out who I was outside of other people, places and things that were defining me. Sometimes, when we are uncertain about who we are, we tend to become a chameleon, or we tend to adapt to whatever environment makes us feel good in the moment. This adaptation justifies our behavior good or bad not even realizing that we are doing this blindly.

What's profound is that when we go through experiences in our life, we can only process those experiences through our own mindset.   I was young and I processed that information from the mind of a child. If I grew up with that mindset, then I grew up with that limiting belief system. Beliefs are conditioned perceptions that are built upon old memories of pain and pleasure. They are essentially assumptions we make about ourselves, about others, and about how we expect things to be in our world. These memories are based on how we have interpreted and emotionalized our experiences over time. By attaching ourselves emotionally to people, events, and circumstances, we effectively build the foundations of our belief systems. These belief systems shape our thoughts and can distort our sense of reality. Think of it like this. We use beliefs as anchors that help express our understanding of the world around us. Ultimately, limiting beliefs can keep you stuck in a negative state of mind and hinder you from living the life you truly desire.

Building one's self-esteem and self-confidence doesn't happen overnight. It took me decades. And, if I'm honest, even today I continue to evolve. Everything my mom said I couldn't do, I made up in my mind that I was going to do it and do it well. My challenge became my mission, my mission became my strategy, and my strategy enabled me to set and achieve my life goals.

Chapter 4
Setting Goals - Start Small…. But Start

Goal setting was critical to achieve the change I desired. I had to learn that it wasn't about starting by pursing the big things in life. It was about showing up daily and doing something. It was about the small, slow, and steady progress to achieve my desired life goals. This is what worked for me. I didn't have the capacity for anything large. Rather than looking at anything big, I broke things down into bite size pieces. I knew the result I desired but didn't know how to get there. I saw the picture but didn't see the strategies and actions required to manifest them.

I Wanted Better

I desired to do better and be better than my current state at that time in my life. After the desire I had to then, create an image of what my goal was to be. I had to ask myself how would I know when I have reached my destination? What would it look like? What would it feel like? How would I communicate it? Once I created the image in my mind, I started thinking about the one thing I could do to move towards that image to accomplish it. I didn't realize it at the time, but I was setting goals. What could I do in 30-days or less, 90-days, a year? I looked at it from the perspective of what can I do today that will put me on the path to get the image I have created.

Ties That Bind

When I started to set my goals, I broke them up into categories – personal, professional, and spiritual. You might have other categories., Be as specific as possible. I examined anything that would hinder me from accomplishing my goals. Was I hindering myself? If so, how? What within me was creating barriers to achieving my goals? Was I allowing someone else's words and opinions to control what was best for me? Was that hindrance rooted in facts or an opinion or personal perception. Because of the way I was raised as a child, I was always made to feel that I wasn't strong enough or I couldn't do anything without the assistance from someone else. I believed I didn't have the mental or cognitive capacity to do things on my own. This was my mindset at the time, but I knew there was more. On some level I knew that I was a creative being. Despite what I was being told, I knew deep down within myself that there was this creative side to me. I just needed to strategize using a method of brainstorming ideas to take off the limits I was putting on myself. Let me pause here to encourage you if you have not done so already to purchase a copy of the "Finding *Joy in Your Mourning Workbook*". In it I walk you through the S.M.A.R.T goal-setting activity to help you navigate through the goal-setting process for success.

Whose Your Cheerleader

There was a woman over our youth ministry at the church I attended growing up. She was the first person to speak contrary to what I had come to believe about myself. She spoke to my potential and what I previously thought to be impossible suddenly became possible in my own eyes. It was this encounter and many others along my life journey that started connecting the dots of purpose for me.

Sometimes you need someone to shine the light in the dark place. Once the light turns on, you can see what's there. Yes, it was easier to focus on the negative versus the positive; to focus on what was happening versus what was not happening. For some people, they get a cheerleader early in life from a parent, family member or teacher; but some get it later in life and there are some that may not necessarily have that at all but that's when you get to a place where you tell yourself that there is something greater or better on the inside of me and you cheer for yourself.

Once I got a new perspective of what's possible, I soon realized that I also had to encourage myself to move towards those possibilities. I had to be my biggest cheerleader. You wake up in the morning and that's another opportunity to start again. Show up daily, do something and start small! This is what helped me. Just being grateful to wake up. I had movement in my limbs and breath in my body. And most important It was the realization that regardless of what happened the day before, I had an opportunity to start again. Each day that I woke up, I chose to do something different than I had done the day before. Every day I found one thing that made feel good about myself. It didn't matter how big or small it was. I found that one thing and began taking small steps.

Changing My Perspective

I had to stop looking at what was going wrong in my life and make a conscious effort to start being grateful for what was right and good in it. My thoughts were all over the place. I woke up every day when my son and husband didn't have that opportunity. It's easy to focus on the bad things in life rather than acknowledging the good things in your life. But it's the focus on those bad things that keeps you bound with an inability to move forward.

Taking it day by day became my norm. Sometimes, it was hour by hour. I simply took one-step at a time, focusing on things that were achievable. For me, my journey began with the goal to be able to get up out of the bed. I might have gotten out of bed and went to lay on the sofa all day, but I achieved my goal. You must be ok with the small victories. I don't know where we learned in life that small is bad. Remember, the adage, "don't despise small beginnings." It's a timeless way of thinking about some things in life. We forget that in a seed, something big can grow and reproduce. It is in the nature of the seed to produce after its own kind. What seeds are you planting in your life by way of spoken words, limiting thoughts and self-defeating behavior? Fear or faith? Trust or doubt? Can or can't? Will or won't? You have the potential within you to reproduce after your own kind. The question is what seeds(knowledge) are you planting inside of you and what are the seeds producing?

My Life Is Not in Vain

Our lives are not in vain. Our experiences are steps in the journey called destiny. I believe that what we experience are previews of coming attractions. What I mean is that your life journey has taught you valuable lessons and you've gained wisdom along the way. That wisdom is now the answer to someone else's problem you have yet to meet. All that we experience in life can help someone else grow and heal. I got to a place where I accepted that my first husband and son had been called to heaven, but I was still here. Why? Surely God had another plan for me on Earth because my husband and child, the thing I always desired in my life, had now been called to heaven. So, I had to fulfill my "BE" ing and purpose in this world, or their life would be in vain. I realized that I am still here because there is more for me to do. This is what I believe for me. That's why I press on because I refuse to allow their significance in my life to be in vain. Each person who has been a part of my life journey has added value to who I am now and to who I am to become. It is me using all the wisdom and knowledge gained from my life experiences good and bad to find my place called purpose and to live a life of fulfillment and joy.

It's About Strategy

With any goal you set, it is going to require a strategy that you put in place to achieve it. Sometimes through those steps you may have to make revisions and changes. The key is to keep going, don't stop.

Set realistic timeframes to meet those goals – if you have challenges believing that you can accomplish your desired goals remember to start small – starting with those things you know you can do within 30-days or less. Start with bite sizes before you work up to the big stuff. Once a timeframe is identified, then write it down – journal, post-its, whatever works for you. For me, I found writing it down somewhere allowed me to see it. It was tangible and very helpful. It served as a subliminal message to keep me on track. Remember, goals are often difficult to achieve because we don't write them down.

Like a computer, our brain can only process so much information at a time. If your brain is already infected with a low self-esteem virus, an insecurity virus or fear virus, you are already working from a deficit. So, writing it down allows you to see tangibly what your mind can't perceive. I can tell myself, "I have so much to do, but I'm not accomplishing anything." But if I write things down and check things off, I have something in front of me that shows what I've accomplished. It shifts my thinking from my opinion to concrete facts which helps me to minimize stress.

Managing My Time Wisely

Writing goals down enables you to identify strategies that will help you move through your process to get to the finish line. In this modern age of technology, you can set alarms on your phone. You can talk to "Alexa" and ask her to remind you to "work on this strategy today" and to really make the effort to do what you say you are going to do. We know that things in life happen unexpectedly but deal with the urgent matter at hand and don't beat yourself up about not achieving that goal or not working on that strategy. How did you deal with that urgent matter and was that taken care of? Did you rise to the occasion? For example, perhaps your goal was to go to the gym, but on the way, you got a flat tire and couldn't go. So instead of focusing on the fact that you didn't make it to the gym, the urgent matter was to get the tire fixed. Life will always throw curve balls and shifting priorities is a part of life. The important thing is, did you accomplish what you needed to do today? It may seem insignificant but in the process of battling with building up self, everything matters.

Celebrate The Small Things

Every step of your goal setting process should be celebrated when you complete it. No matter what, celebrating every step of the way ultimately builds you up and encourages you to keep going. When you get stuck resist telling yourself the following things:

- o When you say, "This always happens!" What you are truly saying is that there will "NEVER" be an opportunity for something different to happen.
- o When you say, "Something bad always happens!" What you are truly saying is nothing good will ever be possible.
- o When you say, "Why do I even try?" What you are truly saying is that you have no possible opportunity to be better than you are right now.

Every day is filled with a goal. When we talk about goal setting, we are talking about the conscious things we want to achieve and that provide fulfillment in life. Don't take the small things like getting out of bed, brushing your teeth, getting outside of the door for granted. For people that are challenged with mental illness, those are major significant things whereas someone else might be trying to get another job, get in college, get another home. You must start with where you are in your process. Self-awareness is key. Be honest about where you are in setting your goals.

Make Sure You Keep It Moving

Goals must be realistic, and everything must be acknowledged. Every opportunity to achieve a goal or the mere fact that there is movement should be acknowledged. You can't just set the goal; you also must know where you are in your process. And part of that requires knowing your strengths and challenges. Make sure your goals are specific, measurable, achievable, realistic & relative, and finally make sure your goals are time sensitive to keep you on task. Recognize that at times your goals might need to be adjusted. That's ok, set a new strategy. The goal is to keep it moving. That's the goal.

I am a firm believer that where your mind is, your body soon follows. If you see it as a problem, your body responds from a posture of defense and anxiety or stress. But if you perceive it as a process, then you come from a position of asking questions. What is it I need to learn in this process? And what do I need to do to get through this process to continue moving forward. Two different perspectives which give you two different results.

Chapter 5
Taking Action

I was setting goals, so in theory, action was taking place in my life. Right? But there were other considerations and elements I had to consider in moving forward to achieve my goals successfully. Happiness comes to those who choose to be happy, but many people wait for permission to be happy or for someone else to make them happy. Permission is nothing more than someone else's approval--but as simple as it is, it keeps you from succeeding and being happy. No one can force you to be happy; no one can force you to accomplish anything you don't want to do. But permission started with me, and it will start with you, for you.

It's About Choice

It was one thing to have my goals staring at me first thing in the morning and all throughout my day. It was another if I didn't take any action towards accomplishing those goals. An example of me choosing to take action was different based on where I was in my process. First, let's take for example the death of my first husband. At that time in my life, I was on autopilot and accepted myself not by who I was within but who I was as defined by the role I was fulfilling as wife. So, when Tony died, I was completely lost. I went into a tailspin not only because he was gone but because I went from wife to widow overnight. I had a new role with no definition, and I did not yet know that greater was living on the inside of me. I just hadn't found it yet. My existence diminished because I couldn't see myself outside of what I did in my role as wife. This mindset caused me to act in ways that were destructive to myself and neglectful of my child. I chose to replace the presence of my husband with drinking, and the thought of me dying was comforting. I was being selfish, I made it all about my pain. I placed no value on me or the fact that if I were incapacitated or God forbid died Cory would have to grow up without his mother and his father. My selfishness was choosing to have my son grow up in the same grief, anger, and loss I experienced most of my life. It was all a destructive solution and a temporary fix.

Fast forward to when my son Cory passed. I chose to acknowledge that although he was my only biological child, I was still a mother figure to several people who no longer had one or who were estranged. My role as mother did not die with my son and my ability to guide, nurture and care for others was an attribute of my character not who I was as "mother". Too often we allow the roles we fulfill to be our sole identity when it is what you do, it's not your only reason for being and existing. When Cory died, I knew I had wisdom to offer. I had been down this road before, and I could not wither and die. God had more for me to do and for every day I drew breathe it was another opportunity to do something that gave me a voice. My paradigm shifted. Life wasn't punishing me. I was placed in a position to give unselfishly to bring about healing and wholeness to others grieving and mourning loss. I chose to get up! I chose to create an image of my new normal and walk in truth. Yes, I was hurting. Yes, I was sad. But no, I was not going to give up and die! I chose to do something with my pain. I chose to do something that allowed me to take back my life. Choosing gave me the authority to live beyond what my grief and mourning was allowing me at that time.

What You Do Counts

Nothing changes until your mindset changes. When your mindset changes your body follows suit. You can rise from any trial if you choose to. Your experiences do not define you as a person. They only provide wisdom and knowledge for you to rise and fight another day until the battle is won. You've got this! Grief does not have you unless you choose to relinquish your power to it. Sure, you might feel better about your life after all the negative thoughts turn over in your head, but you must take action! It's time to take action and watch your life change before your eyes!

Consider this. You must do something for something to happen. Nothing happens until you act. You can't wish or visualize your way to a plate of food, a fancy car, the partner of your dreams, or a successful business. Those things might make it easier for you to act, but you must choose to take action over your thoughts as well as action in your deeds. Let me give you a practical example — water will not run out of a faucet unless you turn the faucet on. You can't even make a paperclip move across your desk without taking action. And you certainly can't get a car to run unless you turn the ignition key.

The more you want to accomplish, the bigger the action you'll need to take. It's not what you _can_ do that matters. It's what you _actually_ _do_ that counts.

Choose to Be Self-Aware

I am now aware of the role my beliefs, values and thoughts play in my personal decision to act. But I wasn't initially. Our beliefs, values, and thoughts influence our behavior. For example, if you believe that you're smart, capable, and good looking, your behavior will be different than if you believe that you're simple minded, incapable, and homely in appearance. None of these things has any actual power in the world, but I believed at one-time they did, and those beliefs influenced my choices and my actions.

Here's the good news. When you take action, you get a result. The small goals I set eventually paid off. I consistently kept moving forward. I consistently kept searching myself for areas that needed improvement and I consistently got back up whenever I fell. When you do nothing, you can become stuck. I've learned that taking action creates additional possibilities in life. When you take action, things change. New opportunities become available. You might meet a new person that can help you get what you want. When you take the first step, the next step appears. Things start happening when you start moving.

The more steps I took, the more my mindset changed, and my behavior changed also. I became strong in a time of weakness. I found joy in my sorrow. I found me.

Chapter 6
The Power of Choice

When we're stuck in the middle of an unhappy or undesirable life circumstance, it often feels as if we don't have any choice at all. We feel trapped in a corner or imprisoned in our unhappy bodies or lives. However, no matter where we are in life there is always a choice about how we move forward. We cannot change what is, but we do have control over our response and the emotional impact – be it negative or positive. You can float through life unconsciously, blaming life circumstances, or others for your hardships. You can feel like a victim of circumstance or a victim of your history; upbringing or whatever you have justified in your own mind. You can go through life quite happily for a while too, making no conscious choices at all, just floating. But all things change, some in an instant, but what you experience today is not what you may experience tomorrow. We are always evolving minute to minute, moment to moment. For this reason, life has no choice but to force you forward; awaiting what a new day will bring.

The traumatic changes happening in my life initially left me feeling like I didn't have a choice. At times when you don't feel like you have a choice, you can become stuck. You don't feel like doing anything. No goals, no action. But those "do nothing" decisions are still a choice. Remember, **NO** decision is a decision!

One of the great things about having the power to choose is that if you don't like where you are in your life right now, you can change it! You're in the driver's seat, and you can actively and intentionally pursue different options for yourself. It's part of your decision-making process to achieve happiness and fulfillment in life.

Acknowledge Your Process

I can now see that the deaths of my husband and son ignited a growth period for me. And yet it was not void of some measure of pain and grief. But it was a part of my life journey. It could not be ignored. I was either going to deal with the change on my terms or allow the change to deal with me leaving me in a declining spiritual, mental, physical, and emotional deficit. You can change outcomes and how you react to situations by your choices. *When we understand who we are and what we are capable of, every bit of that understanding pushes us to "level up."* Choosing to acknowledge the distress I was experiencing opened an opportunity to grow as a woman, as a person. Choosing to acknowledge the grief I felt opened my eyes to begin to see the purpose for all the pain I had experienced. I chose to seek out the gift of understanding to all that I had endured. You have the choice to face your fears, whatever they are, to follow your dreams. Choose to live each day purposefully and not see it go by in a haze of chasing tomorrow. You have a choice and life rewards those who take action.

I noticed that as I began to pay attention to the choices I was making; even the small ones, I was becoming stronger. Awareness was my point of contact. Transformation, healing, and change followed.

As I reflected on my life, I could easily recall that some of the challenging times in my life were due to poor choices. Oh, how I wished I had been a little wiser about some choices I made. But that is life. I eventually became clear, about the steps I needed to take to reach the goals I had set for myself. I'm a huge fan of making lists. A list of resources, alternate choices, weighing pros and cons of any potential choice; long-term implications of that choice; would help define my level of commitment to any choice I made for myself.

It's About Self-Reflection

One of the best ways I find to make better choices is to first think about the impact my *present* actions will have on who I will become later in life. This critical life lesson was an important reminder that I had control over what I did next. Even in the deepest, darkest moments of one's life, you can still choose how you view situations you find yourself in and how you respond.

If you find yourself unsure of what changes you need to make to arrive at better decisions, one thing you can do is to engage in self-reflection. In the Finding *Joy in Your Mourning* workbook, I offer you some self-reflection questions that will help you through your journey. Being self-reflective allows you to dive deep into the recesses of your heart and soul; tune into yourself to discover what barriers or bricks are in the way of you making the right decisions. Most importantly, it will allow you to recognize where you are right now and where you want to be.

Renewing My Mind

For me to take back my power that grief tried to rob from me, I had to uproot some of my old habits and behaviors and replace them with new habits and behaviors. This became a daily process and new way of living my life. My old way of being was dying daily. My power of choice enabled me to be mindful of what I was saying and speaking to my situation – any situation for that matter. Awareness of the confessions I was using to define myself in the growth process became very natural and easy for me. My power of choice allowed me to renew my mind and my thoughts daily. "If I choose better! I act better! And I was starting to live better! These are the confessions I continue to make daily to make the impossible;

possible – turning my fear into faith and eventually helping me to become more resilient.

Today, I make wiser decisions. I trust my intuition and depend on my past and present awareness of myself and my life experiences to make intelligent choices. The best thing is that my smart decisions began to serve me well and still do today!

Chapter 7
Creating an Image of Faith and Belief

I grew up going to church as a little girl, so I "knew of God". I didn't understand at that time in my life that to know of God was distant and external. What I found in my grief was that my spirit needed to "know God". I needed to develop a personal one-on-one relationship with my creator. I needed His love to fill the space within me that I had tried to fill up with people, places, and things, thinking that they in and of themselves would soothe what was aching within me. This simple shift from going to church to being the church was a whole other understanding and journey. It became the game changer that would later prove to be my saving grace when my son died.

Tapping into a spiritual place would lift from me the grip of my grief. For me it was becoming aware that I'm still here and I have not gone through what I've gone through just to suffer in life. There was something greater being worked on inside of me to share with others. There are times in life when something bad happens and creates the most profound sorrow you've ever experienced. It takes a toll on you, and you feel like you'll never overcome it. But there's also the belief that the only way to experience true joy is to first experience the sorrow.

This was a real place for me. I grieved my first husband's death every day for 8 years. It was debilitating. I found myself in such darkness and despair that looking back on it now, I can only describe it as my breaking point! My broken place – my rock bottom! I could no longer overcome my grief on my own. The turning point for me was when I began to look up instead of hanging my head down. I started seeking to heal from the inside out, not the outside in.

A Question of Faith

All emotions are real, especially grieving emotions. You feel pulled in many directions. Finding a way to make sense of it all typically begins with one's faith and the belief system instilled within you when you were a child.

It is very likely that your faith is what has brought you through the darkness thus far. Your faith in the Creator's ability to sustain you should not be overlooked. In the process, if you believe the Creator has kept you going through the worst moments of your life, there is no reason to think you will be alone through the rest of it. Yes, it takes time to overcome challenges but making a conscious effort to separate thinking and reasoning from feeling strengthens your faith. During trying times, it is one's faith that must remain constant, strong, and unwavering. Your faith, if you lean into it, can be the rock that enables you to stay above water. Your faith is the corresponding action to what you're believing for. Faith is doing, thinking, and saying. Faith pushes you to speak God's Word into your challenges and do something.

A Call to Action

Your actions should be based on a strong belief that in the long run, things are going to work out in your favor. When you believe and feel assured that your life is on the path to success, you begin to see opportunities despite the challenges. Preserving and continual growth in your faith and beliefs may require you to incorporate them into the goals you set and the actions you take. Finding someone you trust, perhaps a good friend or family member to support you and hold you accountable is another option while moving through this process. The important thing is to allow your faith and beliefs to ground you and be the focus in making decisions, guiding your choices and ultimately your actions.

It's A Knowing Not a Feeling

It's easy to get swept away in the negative emotions of the day. Though we can't ignore reality, as people of faith we can't allow it to make us hopeless. We get the right attitude when we allow God to renew not just our minds, but the *attitude* of our minds. (Ephesians 4:22-24) If we approach difficulties with an attitude that says, "I will get through this with God's help," it's much easier to face each day. Otherwise, we're trying to swim against the current on our own, and it's only a matter of time before we're carried downstream.

We all know it's easy to love God—or anyone, for that matter—when everything is in perfect rhythm and rhyme. But what happens when things don't go as expected? Do we immediately start blaming God? Do we get frustrated and begin to revisit past ways of thinking and behaving? Do we rehearse past mistakes and poor decisions? This is when we get to prove we believe what we say—that we trust in God and surrender our lives to Him—is what we know and believe. Jesus said all things are possible to those who believe. It is our time-trusted beliefs that get us through the challenging, rough times we encounter in life. (Mark 9:23) Those times will come, but we have hope in our faith and belief system to get us through the tough times and know that we are never alone.

A big part of your spirituality is tied to the core values we live by. Those values guide us and help us in the decisions we make if we allow them to. My daily activity to strengthen my spirituality was to thank God for waking me up each morning. I knew all too well through Tony and Cory's sudden deaths that tomorrow was never promised. This caused me to be mindful and grateful that the simple act of waking up was a gift not a guarantee.

Before starting each day, the moment my eyes opened I expressed gratitude for my breath of life, and I saw each day as an opportunity to do better and be better. My connecting with God from the position of a personal relationship energized me and gave me hope. You see, even the hardest situations become manageable because you know that you are being led by a power higher and greater than yourself. Use your faith as a guidepost while you grow through your issues. It helps you see the possibilities that exist beyond your challenges and your faith helps you grow as an individual and find your place in the universe.

In June of 2016, I became very ill. I was no longer able to work, finances were dwindling and by August of that same year I was burying my only child. It was one hit after another. Before I could recover from one thing, I was hit with something else. It did not make any sense to me. Although

I was faced with a lot I got to a place where I expected God to move on my behalf because that's what He promised in His word. The word truly is living and more than words on a page. It's in our trusting His word that we begin to understand that God will care for us. Surrendering our will allows us to see how he does it. (Psalm 5:3; 27:14; Romans 8:28). I could not do it on my own. I needed to surrender my will and watch God step in and work. Anything less than that was like telling God "I don't need your help I got this." But I didn't.

Faith is about allowing yourself to see beyond what your natural eyes can perceive. In declaring faith in God alone and walking with Him according to His word, you are also declaring that what you see with the natural eyes is not only God's truth but your truth as well. You've undoubtedly heard that "your faith drives your actions, thoughts and beliefs. Intentionally engaging our faith causes one to commit to shut out negativity and allows us to focus on our capabilities.

What Faith Reveals

When we begin to understand how our faith plays a major role in our ability to deal with challenges; we naturally begin to rely on God's word for support, encouragement, and guidance. For me, it became an essential part of my personal action plan to stay strong and continue to fight obstacles that arose in my life. My personal relationship with God unlocked revelations that helped me understand that He was using my problems/challenges to inspect my heart condition, my motives, and my level of faith. He was looking inside of me to see what my "going" through revealed about me. Some lessons I learned through pain and failure. And in some cases what I thought to be punishment was God's protection. I learned by going through my process that some of my problems were a blessing in disguise and that my responses were character builders.

When we are faced with adversity, the question is **"not"** God where are you in the midst of my pain, but rather where are "we" in the middle of God's process? The question is not why me God; but rather God what do you want me to learn in this situation?

The Paradigm Shift

Having faith in Jesus Christ, enables you to see the world and its system differently. The bonus of the Holy Spirit provides guidance and direct access to wisdom and revelation regarding the true nature of things and helps you to see, think, and understand on another level. "The impossible is possible" is not just rhetoric you hear the strong utter in times of distress. It is a reality for you when opposition shows up in your life. Quitting is no longer an option or the innate response.

Your faith and belief systems, renewed and fortified, propel you forward and provoke you to keep moving toward something instead of running from something.

It's Worth the Risk

While I got to a place where I felt secure in my faith, that didn't negate the realization that I would have to also have courage to take risks. Scary? Yes. But with the mental mountains of obstacles and challenges removed from my mind; endless possibilities for my future seemed to abound daily. This change in my reality also left me feeling a lot more inspired, and full of hope for my future. Giving up was not an option. Not anymore. Not ever.

Chapter 8

Healing and Wholeness

My process of healing and becoming whole began with revisiting my past. In doing this what I found was family members recollection and memories were varied and different. Each person's recollection of our childhood was a little different as seen through their lens and life experiences. To understand my early life, I had to talk to my brother and sisters who were there living it with me. This is my process. Not everyone is going to be able or willing to revisit and rehash their past because the trauma is so great. This includes their personal responsibility and accountability. The bottom line is that everything that happened to me or for me, was strategically designed to get me to where I am today. God reveals to us as we are mentally, emotionally, and spiritually equipped to process it. Every day is an opportunity to be your best self despite your beginning.

The Catalyst for Change

The journey to healing from life challenges and loss requires us to transform our thinking about life, relationships, self-love, self-respect, and self-compassion. These life altering events often serve as the catalyst for incredible change and have the potential to motivate us towards empowerment and strength, should we take advantage of the opportunity change brings. Healing and recovery can be a long process, but it is not an impossible one. The effects of traumatic events can be life-changing and undeniable, but a life afterwards is still possible. Wholeness is a complex issue because it involves all of what makes us human – mind, body, soul, emotions, and relationships.

Where Your Mind Is, Your Body Soon Follows

I never gave much thought to my whole body until I became ill. When you are bed bound you have no choice but to think about the state your physically in and the mental and emotional toll fear, stress, and anxiety puts on your body's ability to heal. There were many days where the fear of the unknown and the possibility of the worst happening gripped me. I thought about what I could have done differently. I reflected on many things about my life. But then I got to point where I realized that I only had the energy and mental capacity to deal with the day I was given. I had to process day to day. Whatever the day brought was what I dealt with. The process of change is somewhat like this. When you focus on making little changes daily what you find is that over time you work your way up to bigger ones.

I believe we often focus on our outward experience to define our wholeness within. However, the true lasting work begins from the inside out. You can dress up your outside to allow people to see what you want them to see. But you cannot dress up what is going on inside mentally and emotionally. It's raw, it's undeniable and it can only be contained for so long before it spills out uncontrollably in unhealthy ways through what we speak and how we behave. Our inward transformation is reflected outwardly in all that we say, think and do.

You see your body has spiritual, as well as physical value and it is a gift to you from God, meant for you to offer back to Him in service through His plans and purposes in the earth. The body God made for you is both the place of your personal presence and a temple where the Holy Spirit lives and guides within you. So, it's important to learn how to use your physical being to align with your spiritual being in all that you do when living out your faith and evolving mentally.

Creating an Image of Change

For some people, accepting the negative is easy but it's more difficult to accept the good. The whole person can integrate both the good and bad as part of reality, and this requires relational feedback and personal reflection. When how I saw myself changed, my desires, actions and choices began to change as well. I'm talking about the big picture view of myself. Once this changed, I was able to set goals, make choices to deal with self-imposed imperfections, and learn to be comfortable in my skin. I changed from the inside out. I will always be a work in progress, ever evolving, striving to do and be better – everyday. You see, our life process was designed to all work together for our good and for God's plan and purposes in the earth.

I used to think that being perfect was the goal. I thought "If I'm perfect, everything will be alright in my life." Perfection is not the goal, and no one ever arrives at that place, called Perfect. It is a journey with a greater story unfolding and the imperfections of life are destinations or experiences along the way. Life is not a steady improvement in the right direction. A whole person will have pain, experience struggles and deal with the challenge of broken relationships. But being whole from the inside out will enable you to find comfort within the discomforting points in life. Wholeness from within enables you to get up and press on in hopefulness not hopelessness.

Finding Closure

Holding onto past pain and anguish is a kind of self-inflicted torture that can cause serious health risks as well as emotional scarring. The truth is, when you cling to the past, you're internally changing your present. I didn't realize it at the time, but I truly held onto many emotional pains much longer than I realized. At some point I kept them to justify my behavior so that I didn't have to change. Why should I it wasn't my fault? I kept doing the same things expecting different results and wondering why I kept returning to the same situations and behaviors. I had to accept the fact that life had thrown me curveballs and despite those balls hitting me, and in some cases hitting me hard, I was the only one responsible for the choices I made and the behavior I chose to exhibit because of them. It was how I chose to react to my life circumstances. Healing from these types of hurts is not an easy task, but it can be done with a little effort and self-reflection. Take accountability for the parts that land directly on you and choose to maintain your personal power by not allowing the words and actions of others to define you or the life you have the potential to live.

For me, I first had to identify what exactly was holding me back and talking it out with a close confident or someone I trusted helped me through this process. Getting closure on something that was left open-ended can make a difference. Next, I had to manage the emotions that automatically rise to the surface when confronting painful experiences from my past. Bottling up your emotions is never a good thing. Forgiving yes, forgetting may not happen. However, it is you choosing despite the memory to focus on the lessons learned and growth and wisdom gained rather than the damage done is also a key part of this process of healing.

Forgiving is For You

It may sound easier said than done but forgiving someone can be extremely therapeutic. You are the primary benefactor. Forgiving doesn't absolve a person from their responsibility. That is their work to do. Forgiving gives you your power and permission to move on and rise above what that person said or did. Look at it this way. Unforgiveness gives the other person control over your thoughts and emotions. Forgiveness takes that control back and uses it to become better than you were before. Healing that comes from forgiving transgressions benefit us more than the offender of the hurt. Whether you reach out directly or simply forgive them in thought, make the move to forgive any offense. It's up to you to take control of the pain and take the first step towards making yourself feel better. At the end of the day, it's important to strive rather than to let things stay in the past and allow them to infect your present. Once you learn to forgive you will find it far easier to heal and move on with your life. Making the conscious decision, today, to live your life free from pain and resentment is an experience that you will never forget.

Taking the Limits Off

Another area that I had to consider in my life were self-imposed limitations. To put it simply, self-limiting beliefs are assumptions or perceptions that you've got about yourself and about the way the world works. These assumptions are "self-limiting" because in some way they hold one back from achieving what they may be capable of. And to change anything, you must first identify it. Some limiting beliefs are subconscious and require time and patience within us to really make sure we identify anything that might be hindering our healing process. I limited myself by believing negative things people said to me and about me. As I reflect, they were limited in their own thinking. They had a choking point that could not allow them to see beyond their own limits that they were placing on me and the limits they were placing on themselves. An example of this is when I allowed myself to do just enough in school to get by. I constantly allowed my mother's voice in my head to tell me I wasn't capable. This limited my ability to even try. I believed I was unable to conceive the possibility to do and be more. This fear paralyzed my growth process for years. I had to work through my perceptions of others to decide what it was I wanted to do and to accept that the world would not stop if I tried. You never know what you're capable of until you try. So, I did! I tried and sometimes I was successful and sometimes I had to try harder.

Do You Believe What You See or See What You Believe?

From a very early age, we begin to form beliefs about the world and our place in it, usually by our parents and other dominant figures in our lives. Our brains are very good at spotting patterns and making associations, so we constantly process the stream of information about the world around us and use it to form beliefs. Generally, the purpose of belief formation is to help us understand the world and stay safe. As we get older, we start to form more complex beliefs and can draw on a much wider range of sources such as books, movies, TV advertisements, the behavior of our peers, and so on. Nevertheless, the core beliefs that we formed as young children can be very powerful, and even when we encounter new information or explanations, we often cling to our old beliefs.

These beliefs sometimes playout as self-defeating behaviors. The most powerful thing that you can do is eliminate limiting beliefs and replace them with beliefs that empower you.

You learned about yourself from various sources over the years — tests you took, feedback you received from others, what your parents said to you, and how your peers treated you. And there's a good chance you developed some inaccurate self-limiting beliefs along the way.

Drawing the Line in the Sand

Healing allows us to also form healthy boundaries – those guidelines, rules, or limitations that a person creates to identify for themselves what are reasonable, safe, and permissible ways for other people to behave around them and how they will respond when someone steps outside those limits. The easiest way to think about a boundary is a property line. We have all seen "No Trespassing" signs, which send a clear message that if you violate that boundary, there will be a consequence.

Creating healthy boundaries is work as there are many types of boundaries to consider, but it's also empowering. By recognizing the need to set and enforce limits, you protect your wholeness, your sense of being and ultimately enjoy healthy relationships with friends and family. Unhealthy boundaries cause emotional pain that can lead to dependency, depression, anxiety, and even stress-induced physical illness. A lack of boundaries is like leaving the door to your home unlocked: anyone, including unwelcome guests, can enter at will. On the other hand, having too rigid boundaries can lead to isolation, like living in a locked-up castle surrounded by a mote. No one can get in, and you can't get out. When you have weak emotional boundaries, it's like getting caught in the middle of a hurricane with no protection. You expose yourself to being greatly affected by others' words, thoughts, and actions and end up feeling bruised, wounded, and battered.

Trauma Is Emotional

Emotional trauma can leave you struggling with upsetting emotions, memories, and anxieties that are challenging to overcome. It can also leave you feeling numb, disconnected, and unable to trust other people. When bad things happen, it can take a while to get over the pain and feel safe again. After Tony died, I was always waiting for the other shoe to drop.

But healing and wholeness is possible, whether its trauma from our childhood or something that happened more recently in one's life. Overcoming the trauma and moving towards healing takes time and will happen differently for different people. The goal is to not get stuck in the darkness because you must get up when mourning comes and mourning always comes! So don't judge your own reactions or those of other people as you strive towards healing. Your responses are normal reactions to some abnormal events that have taken place in your life.

Step Up and Take Your Shot

As difficult as it may sound it's important to remember that you control the pace of your healing process. But step up to the plate to take your very best shot at accepting that something happened to cause you grief. Acceptance doesn't have to mean being nonchalant about the pain and hurt, because those are very real. But you can tell yourself that the event has already happened, it is in the past, I will, and I am going to get beyond this and heal. You can tell yourself that every day if necessary. You haven't been given the power to change things that have already occurred, but you can certainly change how you deal with the challenge going forward with the goal of healing in your future!

Finding peace while grieving will be difficult at the beginning, and there are really no rules for how long you should take to heal. However, remember that there's a season for everything. Your feelings of hurt and pain have no plans to last forever unless you give them the authority to. One of the things I used to tell my clients at the County Correctional Center was "have the experience, feel the emotion and then let the emotion go" so that your healing can progress forward, fueled by your thoughts of what's next. Letting the emotions go doesn't dismiss the reality of the experience. But it prevents you from getting stuck in the past and the traumatic moment. Emotions are an energy force that could negatively impact you physically. Your thoughts of health and becoming whole again that empowers you to get past the pain, overcome it and to think about ways to move forward in life.

Before you know it, you will become whole and becoming more resilient will be the focus as you move towards achieving your goals. Healing and becoming whole is the catalyst that positions you to accomplish all you desire.

Chapter 9
Finding My Place Called Purpose

I don't remember how old I was when I became clear about what I wanted to do. And things became even foggier when I try to pinpoint when I knew what I was purposed to do. More important, what was my purpose. I had spent the better part of my early life, navigating through sadness, tragedy, and trauma, and figuring out how to cope and heal from it all.

I didn't start out "walking in my purpose. Or so I thought." I think most people are led to believe that finding your purpose is this skill, assignment, or body of work we were born to fulfill at some point in life. This way of thinking can be discouraging. Especially to someone who has more years behind them then ahead and they have not yet tapped into that thing that answers the question "What Am I Here For?"

Living Your "BE"

Throughout my life journey I was surprised by some of the personal discoveries I learned about myself. I kept my mind open and abandoned self-limiting thoughts. I made cognizant choices and tried to reduce the temptation to feel overwhelmed. I changed my assumptions, remembering to focus on my past accomplishments. I made sure my plans were realistic. Sure, I had big ideas, but the small steps and setting goals kept me on target to meet my goals. Something else that helped me was pursing my purpose daily. Each day I would figure out something I could do to bring me closer to my goals. You see, I have found the secret and solved the mystery of the proverbial question, "what is my purpose?" When I discovered it, it was so profound and yet it was such a simplistic answer. Do you want to know what it is? Are you truly ready to unlock this mystery to self-fulfillment?

"BE"! That's it, "BE". Now I know you're wondering how two little letters can solve such a big mystery. Well, I'm going to tell you. Your purpose is to be the very best version of yourself. It is the embodiment of your skills, your gifts and talents rolled into the uniqueness called you. When you pursue your best self the opportunities to do what you do find you and present themselves. Let's look at it this way. Everything I have been through and done in my life journey has imparted wisdom and knowledge to position me to do exactly what I'm doing now in life. I am a life coach, an inspirational speaker, and an author. But to "get to this place" I had to "go through" my process.

The key was consistency. No, that's not always easy either. Sometimes I found myself taking three steps forward only to take two steps back. I got complacent about using the tools in my "empowerment toolbox." I thought "I'm good now. I've got this." But just like a muscle can atrophy over time because it's not used and exercised, our growth can do the same. Your tools (self-awareness, proactive thinking, positive self-talk, goal setting and exercising choice strategies) only work consistently when you use them. They don't fix what was wrong. The tools you gain help you to maintain your ability to get up, keep it moving and thrive. I had to create a desire to desire becoming my best self. Not to be a life coach, an inspirational speaker, or an author. But in an effort to "BE" whole, "BE" resilient and "BE" creative. When I embraced my "BEING" the work of purpose presented itself. Small victories and completing small tasks added up and built momentum, but I had to evaluate my progress, dodge distractions, and adjust along the way.

Throughout my journey, it was a challenge to balance my pursuit of "BE"-ing with some action that I needed to take to fulfill an external display of who I thought I was. I didn't want to miss an opportunity, but I also didn't want to get ahead of myself either. It was an ongoing challenge. When I re-directed my focus inward, the fullness of my "BE"-ing overflowed outward. Without trying, it was seen. It oozed out of my walk, my talk and how I thought.

'BE" your best self and allow the work of purpose to pursue you organically. Seeking out support from friends, family and mentors are a plus in this process. Connecting with a partner who shares your values and vision can be a tremendous asset, especially when you are just simply trying to figure out what your "BE" (purpose) is.

Is It a Talent or a Skill?

Is it my ability to sing, draw, or dance? Every person possesses certain skills and talent, that makes us different from others. We often use the terms talent and skill interchangeably, without understanding they are very different from one another. Talent is something that one is born with; it is your natural ability to do something without really thinking about it. Skill, on the other hand, is something that you acquire after putting in a lot of hard work to learn how to do it. What comes naturally for me, may not be as effortless for someone else, but that doesn't mean they couldn't acquire that skill.

I initially focused on those skills/talents where I naturally shined, and I loved doing it. I pondered the things I was drawn to and that made me feel unique and special.

I was working and enjoying my career as a Correctional Treatment Coordinator, but I also had other interests not tied to my "day job." All the things I enjoyed externally did not and could not fix what was going on inside of me. Remember this process works from the inside out, not the outside in. As an example, a car may look good on the outside but if the engine is damaged it's not going to perform at it designed best. There are plenty of people who are dressed up on the outside and messed up on the inside.

We feel the most alive about life when we find balance with what we are passionately great at doing. Remember, what we were created for was to "BE' our best selves. When we do something that comes naturally to us—a talent— we are fully expressing a part of our whole self. Examining our talents and other qualities shed light on what aspects of ourselves we can offer for greater service to humanity, which also happens to be the same gifts that bring the work of purpose to life.

The True You

I am a firm believer that our works of purpose are divinely aligned with those things that make us unique. Our dreams are calling us. The true you, authentically and unapologetically! Often the key to unlocking both passion and the specific work of purpose is to allow ourselves to remember our dreams and go for them! Dreams articulate those things we would want if we could have anything and those things we would do if we had the opportunity.

They can also be one's passions that get your blood boiling. Those issues that tug at our heart strings because we care about them. Our values and ideals about life drive us towards finding ways to make the world better, often in specific ways. We find ourselves pondering how we can change the world and how we can "BE", the change we want to see in the world. Tuning into these greater values can unleash our passion.

Finding one's purpose might also require being open to being in a different place. Stepping out of one's comfort zone.

Allowing our self to experience things we might have avoided for whatever reason. Imagine there is a favorite sport you want to play. You can't play unless you get in the game. Sitting on the sideline leaves you as a spectator in the action of something you love.

Finding your work of purpose will shed light on those things you should be doing? Perhaps it's a business. It could be a higher calling in ministry. It could have you on the front lines of a socio-economic issue. Focus on your "Be-ing" and the work will find you. I came to believe I had something to say, but it was my insecurity about my ability to even write that almost talked me out of writing this book. It was me doing my "BE" that positioned me to be introduced to my co-writer and publisher Shelly Burgess. But just as it happened for me it happened for Shelly simultaneously. Living our "BE" is reciprocal.

It is the gift that is given just as much as it is received. Remember, we are the answer to someone's challenge or need. Our willingness to do our self-work enables us to make destiny connections throughout our life journey. Our readiness determines the time and place and our life lessons and wisdom prepare us for the meeting.

Chapter 10
Divine Connections

Life is so complex that we sometimes miss patterns, circumstances and divine connections that have truly influenced us because we are so focused on getting by or thinking about the past or future. If we were to take a piece of paper and list out all the people who have helped shape and influence our lives, we would be surprised at how vast the list is. The relationships would vary in deep and meaningful ways. But whether it was a stranger we saw one-time or a parent or spouse, every connection adds meaning to our life. The goal is to understand the individual parts these connections play in the big picture of our lives.

There's Power in A Story

For centuries, telling a story has long been the way we learned about and shaped the core values we live by in every culture of the world. Whether we are aware of it or not, this has been very true in each of our lives and there is great value in laying it out and looking for patterns and themes in our history. All of life can be experienced as a story. Stories engage our heart, emotions, and our imagination, not just the mind. We are shaped by the stories we live. The important thing is to take the time to understand them or not.

Telling your story can bring you to a place of brokenness, to true repentance and ultimately healing and wholeness. Telling your story helps us find our authentic self. Sometimes we can get stuck simply telling what happened. It's important to tell how you overcame it to position yourself to help others who are actively in what you've come out of. You now become the answer to someone's situation or challenge.

Facing our deepest hurts and disappointments in life can lead to the 'poverty of spirit' that is the foundation of all true change.

"Poverty of Spirit" is the thought that we are less than, not enough or incapable of making it through. It's an "I Can't" perception. We can face our pains. forgive those who have hurt us, forgive God for having allowed it to happen, and repent of our self-centered attempts to use this pain as an excuse to not love God and others well. It clarifies vision and our purpose in life.

Knowing of God is the knowledge of religion. Knowing God, and there is a difference, speaks to our personal relationship with a sovereign being. Look at it this way, think of people you know. When you know of someone you are not invested in getting to know what drives them or makes them tick. When you know of God, He is far off and untouchable and unreachable. When you know God, He is right there with you in every situation. He is making a way out, making provision and through His word, He is giving you guidance and instruction for any situation that life may bring. It's in knowing God where our trust and belief is evident, and it is our "go to" in times of trouble. Knowing God is to know His character and to know that HE knew you before you were created (Jeremiah 1:5; Psalm 139:13-18) and provided provision for who you are to BE in the earth. This is the ultimate divine connection that walks us into our true purpose and calling.

God was laying sovereign foundations in our lives even before we knew Him personally. Ephesians 2:10 says that we are 'His workmanship - His poem or work of art.' He has a plan for our lives; a unique calling that He wants us to fulfill. Reflecting prayerfully on our lives helps us to discern His threads in the tapestry of our unique designs.

By looking at your life on a timeline you can see it more objectively. You may notice a pattern or a series of experiences that led you to where you are today. Understanding this, you may notice your life has been leading you towards something meaningful, powerful, and purposeful. If you can embrace the plot of the story, you may be able to decipher where it's going. While reflecting on the experiences of your life, if your first thoughts of the future are negative or limiting it is important to note that you can change and create what you want in life by finding a greater purpose after the experiences. Once something that was unconscious becomes *conscious*, you have *choice*.

Childhood Influences

Society and how we were raised as a child influences a great deal of who we are in many ways. Some people don't deny those things have an impact, but some people think the effect is minimal and resist believing that their actions and beliefs were formed by the influence of other people good or bad. If we take time to reflect on how much of what we do and think did not originate as our own idea and let go of things that do not serve us, we are free to embrace beliefs and life choices that genuinely resonate with who we truly are and the life that we want to live.

It's All About Connections

Everybody contributes something to the world through a group, your family, a sports team, a community, or organization your placed in. The connections you make are unique to the circles of influence your called to function in. My divine connections have evolved over the course of my life. All have shaped me into the person I am today, and all were purposeful.

When certain people come into our lives, we sometimes do not realize what their purpose is. In the moment, it is sometimes hard to grasp their presence, or perhaps we have such a good time we forget to step back and appreciate the now. These connections that exist can help us navigate, appreciate, and open our bandwidth for viewing different moments and stages in life.

What you will notice is that there are certain times in life, the universe is nudging you towards something, and this is generally when "divine connections" tend to find one another. It could be during a difficult or positive time in your life, or when you might need to just level up! Divine connections can show up unexpectedly and often be camouflaged in adversity. The next time you question why something is happening, look back and remember that some connections come for a specific reason to help us with a particular mission or life lesson. You never really outgrow anyone; two people simply choose to continue their respective life journeys. When I meet someone, the question I ask myself is how can I add value to their life or how they can they add value to mine? We are all important to God and to the people we are called to serve. Don't discount coincidences. These are opportunities for you, to BE authentically you in the earth. At the end of the day, the next time you meet someone, ask God how you can be a blessing to them. Just show up and be available.

Epilogue

One of the major obstacles to maximizing success and happiness in life is a lack of self-awareness. You know your friends' flaws better than they do. It's human nature to not have an accurate view of yourself. Some are more aware than others. Any *Emotional Intelligence IQ* test will give insight into yourself as well as those around you. We'd rather stick our heads in the sand and remain oblivious to our shortcomings. We'd prefer to believe that we're unlucky instead of acknowledging that perhaps we just didn't take the right approach. Unfortunately, the implications of not being self-aware is a problem. If we can't see ourselves and our behaviors accurately, how can you grow and evolve optimally?

If you're brave enough to develop a keen sense of self-awareness, you'll be more likely to have a successful and rewarding life. Self-awareness will allow you to regain and sustain mastery over your life and find joy amid mourning! Grief is not just the death of a loved one, but it is the loss of anything or anyone that we are emotionally and mentally tied to or invested in. These losses cause us to behave (mourn) in various ways. We have the ability as human beings to choose how we respond and how we move forward.

www.ingramcontent.com/pod-product-compliance
Lightning Source LLC
Chambersburg PA
CBHW070832160726
48004CB00001B/350